WITHDRAWN

STATE PROFILES
NEBRASKA

BY RACHEL GRACK

BELLWETHER MEDIA • MINNEAPOLIS, MN

Blastoff! Discovery launches a new mission: reading to learn. Filled with facts and features, each book offers you an exciting new world to explore!

BLASTOFF! UNIVERSE

BLASTOFF! Beginners — GRADE K

BLASTOFF! READERS — GRADES 1-3

BLASTOFF! DISCOVERY — GRADE 4

This edition first published in 2022 by Bellwether Media, Inc.

No part of this publication may be reproduced in whole or in part without written permission of the publisher.
For information regarding permission, write to Bellwether Media, Inc., Attention: Permissions Department,
6012 Blue Circle Drive, Minnetonka, MN 55343.

Library of Congress Cataloging-in-Publication Data

Names: Koestler-Grack, Rachel A., 1973- author.
Title: Nebraska / by Rachel Grack.
Description: Minneapolis, MN : Bellwether Media, Inc., 2022. |
    Series: Blastoff! Discovery: State profiles | Includes bibliographical
    references and index. | Audience: Ages 7-13 | Audience: Grades
    4-6 | Summary: "Engaging images accompany information
    about Nebraska. The combination of high-interest subject matter
    and narrative text is intended for students in grades 3 through 8"–
    Provided by publisher.
Identifiers: LCCN 2021019685 (print) | LCCN 2021019686 (ebook)
    | ISBN 9781644873328 (library binding) |
    ISBN 9781648341755 (ebook)
Subjects: LCSH: Nebraska–Juvenile literature.
Classification: LCC F666.3 .K64 2022 (print) | LCC F666.3 (ebook)
    | DDC 978.2–dc23
LC record available at https://lccn.loc.gov/2021019685
LC ebook record available at https://lccn.loc.gov/2021019686

Text copyright © 2022 by Bellwether Media, Inc. BLASTOFF!
DISCOVERY and associated logos are trademarks and/or registered trademarks of Bellwether Media, Inc.

Editor: Betsy Rathburn   Designer: Andrea Schneider

Printed in the United States of America, North Mankato, MN.

TABLE OF CONTENTS

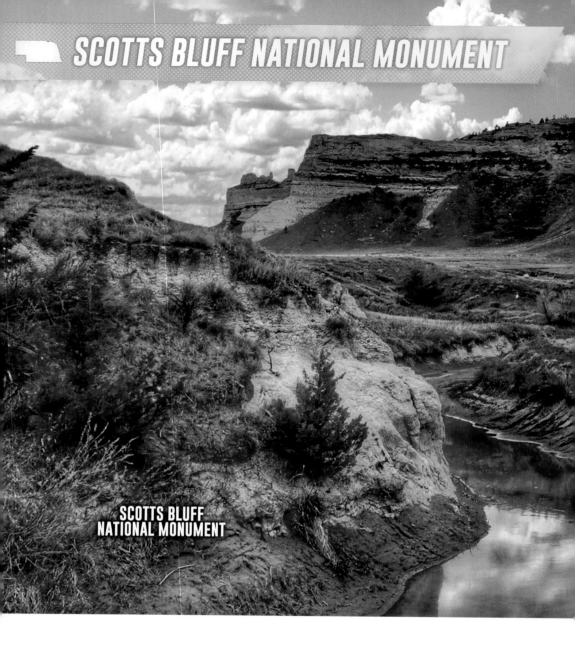

SCOTTS BLUFF
NATIONAL MONUMENT

A family is ready to explore Scotts Bluff National Monument. Around them, rocky **bluffs** rise from the wide-open **prairie**. Prairie grasses dance and bow in the breeze. The wind brings some relief from the hot summer sun. Under the big, blue sky, the family sets off down a dusty trail.

ASHFALL FOSSIL BEDS STATE HISTORICAL PARK

CHIMNEY ROCK

FORT KEARNY

HENRY DOORLY ZOO AND AQUARIUM

The trail takes the family to a covered wagon. More than 150 years ago, horse-drawn wagons like this one transported people through the area on the Oregon Trail! Another trail takes the family high above the prairie. They take in the view of the North Platte River below. Welcome to Nebraska!

Nebraska is in the **Great Plains** region of the **Midwest**. It is the 16th largest state, covering 77,348 square miles (200,330 square kilometers). Wyoming is to the west. South Dakota sits along the northern border. The Missouri River creates the eastern border with Iowa and Missouri. Kansas lies to the south. Colorado cuts into the southwestern corner, creating Nebraska's panhandle.

Most of Nebraska's major cities are in the east. Lincoln, the state capital, lies in the southeastern corner. Omaha, the largest city, is along the Missouri River. Grand Island is on the Platte River in central Nebraska.

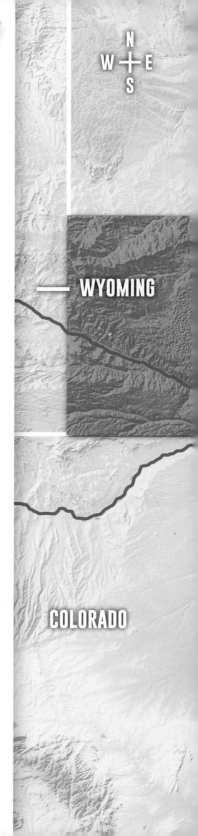

WYOMING

COLORADO

SOUTH DAKOTA

MISSOURI
RIVER

IOWA

NEBRASKA

PLATTE
RIVER

OMAHA

LEXINGTON

GRAND ISLAND

LINCOLN

BELLEVUE

MISSOURI

KANSAS

MISSOURI RIVER

The Missouri River is the longest river in North America. It flows more than 2,300 miles (3,701 kilometers)!

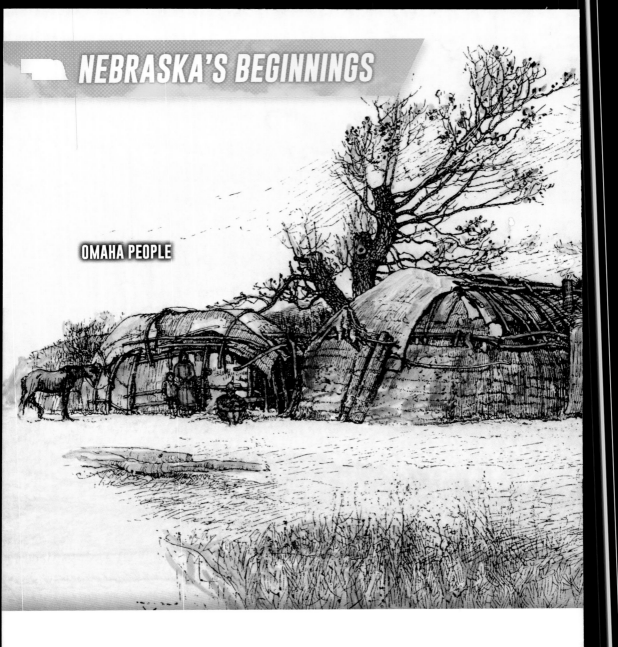

OMAHA PEOPLE

People first came to Nebraska more than 10,000 years ago. Many Native American tribes formed. Villages of Omaha, Oto, Pawnee, and Ponca people farmed eastern and central Nebraska. The Sioux, Cheyenne, Arapahoe, and Comanche tribes hunted bison in the west.

In 1803, the United States bought Nebraska from France in the **Louisiana Purchase**. Starting in the 1830s, thousands of people began traveling west through Nebraska on the Oregon Trail. In 1863, **settlers** rushed to claim free land in Nebraska offered by the government. Four years later, Nebraska became the 37th state. By the 1880s, few of Nebraska's Native Americans lived on their original land.

NATIVE PEOPLES OF NEBRASKA

SANTEE SIOUX

- Original lands in northern Minnesota
- More than 2,600 members today
- Also called Dakota

OMAHA

- Original lands in the Ohio River Valley, later moving west into Iowa
- More than 5,000 members today

WINNEBAGO

- Original lands across Wisconsin and Illinois
- More than 4,000 members today
- Also called Ho-Chunk

PONCA

- Original lands in northeastern Nebraska
- About 4,200 members today

Eastern Nebraska is mainly rolling, hilly prairie. In the west, the hills flatten into the treeless fields of the Great Plains. The rocky Pine Ridge area cuts across the northwestern corner of the state. The northwest is also home to the Sand Hills. This area of hills and

PLATTE RIVER

☐ PINE RIDGE ■ SAND HILLS

grasslands spreads into north-central Nebraska. Nebraska's most important river, the Platte, winds through southern Nebraska.

CHIMNEY ROCK

Chimney Rock is a famous rock formation in western Nebraska. It rises more than 300 feet (91 meters) above the ground!

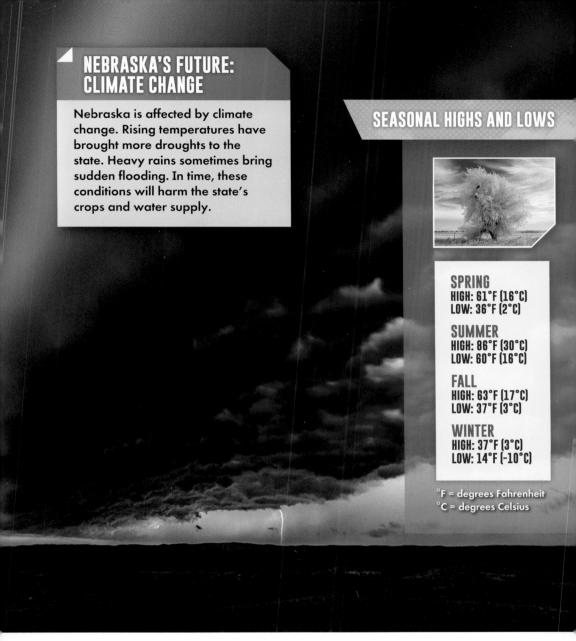

NEBRASKA'S FUTURE: CLIMATE CHANGE

Nebraska is affected by climate change. Rising temperatures have brought more droughts to the state. Heavy rains sometimes bring sudden flooding. In time, these conditions will harm the state's crops and water supply.

SEASONAL HIGHS AND LOWS

SPRING
HIGH: 61°F (16°C)
LOW: 36°F (2°C)

SUMMER
HIGH: 86°F (30°C)
LOW: 60°F (16°C)

FALL
HIGH: 63°F (17°C)
LOW: 37°F (3°C)

WINTER
HIGH: 37°F (3°C)
LOW: 14°F (-10°C)

°F = degrees Fahrenheit
°C = degrees Celsius

Nebraska experiences all four seasons. In the east, winters bring heavy snowfall and cold winds. Western Nebraska is more dry. Summers are hot throughout the state. Thunderstorms often bring tornadoes.

Across Nebraska's prairies, coyotes slink through tall grasses. They hunt jackrabbits and kangaroo rats. Prairie dogs poke their heads out of their underground homes. Prairie chickens race along the ground, and meadowlarks soar through the sky. Along streams, ducks, geese, pheasants, and wild turkeys find nesting spots.

Pronghorn roam Nebraska's grassy Sand Hills in search of food. Elk wander the state's rocky slopes. Mountain lions crouch on cliffs above them, ready to pounce. They also stalk deer, foxes, and raccoons. In the brush, rattlesnakes shake their tails to scare away passing enemies.

COYOTE

ORD'S KANGAROO RAT

WILD TURKEY

TIMBER RATTLESNAKE

12

MOUNTAIN LION

BLACK-TAILED PRAIRIE DOG

Life Span: up to 8 years
Status: least concern

black-tailed prairie dog range = ▪

LEAST CONCERN	NEAR THREATENED	VULNERABLE	ENDANGERED	CRITICALLY ENDANGERED	EXTINCT IN THE WILD	EXTINCT

13

Nebraska has a population of around 2 million people. About 7 out of 10 Nebraskans live in cities. Most live in Omaha and Lincoln. Some Native Americans live on **reservations** in northeastern and southeastern Nebraska.

OMAHA

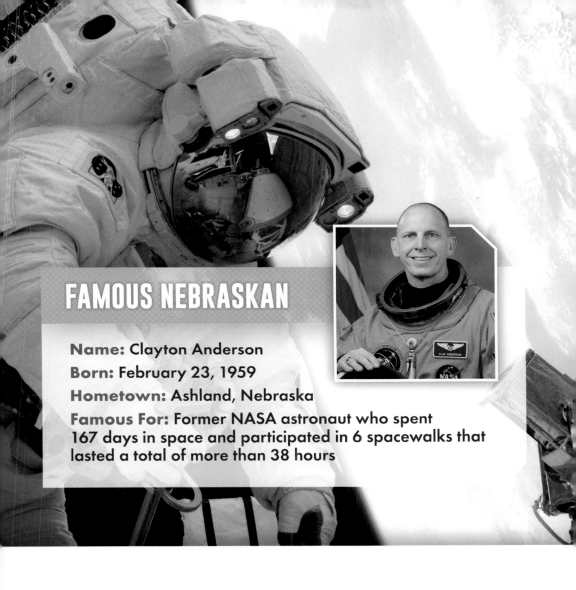

FAMOUS NEBRASKAN

Name: Clayton Anderson
Born: February 23, 1959
Hometown: Ashland, Nebraska
Famous For: Former NASA astronaut who spent 167 days in space and participated in 6 spacewalks that lasted a total of more than 38 hours

Nebraska's early settlers were mostly German. Today, residents have many different backgrounds. Most Nebraskans have European roots. Around 1 in 10 Nebraskans is Hispanic. Smaller numbers are African American or Black, Asian American, or Native American. Many immigrants are moving to Nebraska, too. Newcomers are from Mexico, Guatemala, India, Myanmar (Burma), and Vietnam.

CAPITOL BUILDING

Lincoln is Nebraska's capital city. It was founded as Lancaster in 1856. People settled there to mine salt. In 1867, the city was renamed to Lincoln and chosen as the state capital. Lincoln soon became a railroad center. By the 1890s, 19 different rail routes crisscrossed the city.

RAIL YARD

Today, Lincoln is the second-largest city in Nebraska. Many people work and go to school at the University of Nebraska. Lincoln is full of **cultural** activities, too. People view art from around the world at the Sheldon Museum of Arts. They stroll through colorful flowers at the Sunken Garden or visit animals at the Lincoln Children's Zoo!

SUNKEN GARDEN

INDUSTRY

Since Nebraska's early days, farming has been the state's most important industry. Today, corn is its top crop. Farmers also grow alfalfa hay and beans. Livestock farmers raise cattle, hogs, and chickens. Most of the state is farmland!

NEBRASKA'S FUTURE: SKILLED WORKERS

Nebraska is having a hard time finding skilled workers for certain jobs. People need special training to fill these positions. But many young people are leaving the state. The state may try to attract students by paying for college or offering good jobs.

18

Most Nebraskans hold service jobs. Many work in schools or stores. Insurance is a major industry in Omaha. Other Nebraskans work in manufacturing. The state's top products are processed foods, machinery, chemicals, metals, and transportation equipment. Natural resources are also important. Nebraska's most important resources are petroleum, sand, gravel, and limestone.

INVENTED IN NEBRASKA

LOCKING PLIERS

Date Invented: patented in 1924

Inventor: William Petersen

ARBOR DAY

Date Invented: 1872

Inventor: Julius Sterling Morton

KOOL-AID

Date Invented: 1927

Inventor: Edwin Perkins

FROZEN TV DINNERS

Date Invented: 1953

Inventor: Swanson

SCHOOL LUNCH FAVORITE

Many people serve chili with cinnamon rolls in Nebraska. This unusual combination was once commonly served in school lunches. It has become a favorite meal!

Nebraskans love popcorn balls. These treats are made of popcorn stuck together with sugar syrup. Reuben sandwiches were invented by a chef in Omaha. They are made with corned beef, sauerkraut, Swiss cheese, and dressing on rye bread. *Runzas*, bread pockets stuffed with beef and sauerkraut, are also popular. They were brought to Nebraska by German-Russian immigrants.

Several kinds of ice cream were invented in Nebraska. Butter brickle is made with toffee pieces in ice cream. Tin roof sundaes began in Nebraska, too. Ice cream is covered with chocolate and peanuts! In Potter, Nebraska, they also include marshmallow crème and chocolate ice cream!

RUNZA

POPCORN BALLS

12 SERVINGS

Have an adult help you make this popular Nebraska treat!

INGREDIENTS

12 cups popped popcorn

1 cup granulated sugar

1/2 cup corn syrup

1/4 cup butter

1/2 teaspoon salt

1 teaspoon vanilla extract

1/2 teaspoon baking soda

nonstick cooking spray

DIRECTIONS

1. Place the popped popcorn in a large container.

2. In a large saucepan, combine the sugar, corn syrup, butter, and salt. Bring to a boil.

3. Remove the mixture from heat. Stir in the vanilla extract and baking soda.

4. Pour the syrup over the popcorn and stir to coat.

5. Let the popcorn cool slightly until it can be safely touched.

6. Spray your hands with the nonstick cooking spray. Use your hands to form the popcorn into balls. Work quickly so that the mixture does not harden.

7. Let the popcorn balls cool completely. Enjoy!

OMAHA STORM CHASERS

Nebraska's most popular sport is college football! People love cheering for the University of Nebraska Cornhuskers. The Omaha Storm Chasers baseball team plays in the minor leagues. Rodeo is another popular sport.

RODEO

Many Nebraskans enjoy art. The Joslyn Art Museum attracts people to its galleries and sculpture gardens. Theater and music performances are also common. Some of Nebraska's biggest cities have public art displays. They are known for life-size statues and huge outdoor paintings. People also enjoy hiking in Nebraska's parks and fishing or boating in its lakes.

JOSLYN ART MUSEUM

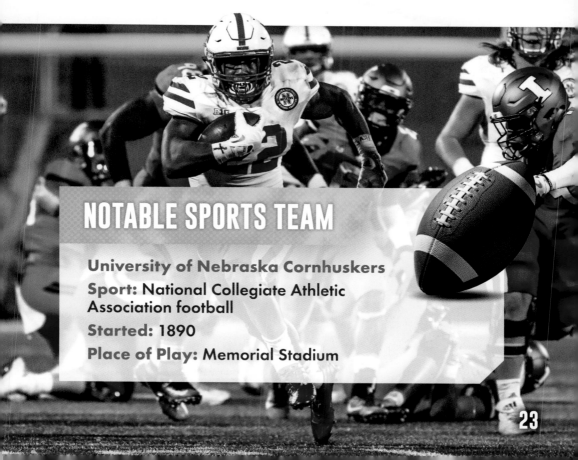

NOTABLE SPORTS TEAM

University of Nebraska Cornhuskers

Sport: National Collegiate Athletic Association football

Started: 1890

Place of Play: Memorial Stadium

Each July, Nebraskans celebrate Oregon Trail Days in Gering. This festival honors those who crossed the state by covered wagon in the 1800s. The Big Rodeo in Burwell is another popular July event. Nebraskans gather to watch bull riding, steer wrestling, and barrel racing.

Many Nebraska festivals celebrate the state's many cultures. July brings the Winnebago Homecoming **Powwow** and Celebration. People enjoy **traditional** Winnebago music and dancing. In August, the Czech Days festival celebrates Czech **heritage** with food, dancing, and crafts. There is a lot to celebrate in Nebraska!

CZECH DAYS FESTIVAL

WINNEBAGO HOMECOMING POWWOW AND CELEBRATION

1863
Thousands of settlers arrive in Nebraska to claim land under the Homestead Act

1803
The United States buys present-day Nebraska from France in the Louisiana Purchase

1930s
Severe drought leads parts of Nebraska to become part of the Dust Bowl

1804
Lewis and Clark explore Nebraska

1867
Nebraska becomes the 37th state, and Lincoln is chosen as the capital

1986

Nebraska elects
Kay A. Orr as its first
female governor

2019

A heavy blizzard leads
to costly flooding across
western Nebraska

2011

The Missouri River
floods eastern
Nebraska

1936

Construction begins
on Kingsley Dam near
Ogallala, forming the Lake
McConaughy reservoir

27

Nickname: The Cornhusker State

Motto: Equality Before the Law

Date of Statehood: March 1, 1867 (the 37th state)

Capital City: Lincoln ★

Other Major Cities: Omaha, Bellevue, Grand Island

Area: 77,348 square miles (200,330 square kilometers); Nebraska is the 16th largest state.

Population

1,961,504
(2020)

STATE FLAG

Nebraska's flag is dark blue. In the center is a gold and silver seal. Around the top, the seal says "Great Seal of the State of Nebraska." The bottom of the seal shows Nebraska's date of statehood. In the middle, a blacksmith hammers an anvil. Behind him, a small cabin represents Nebraska's early settlers and farming. Near the cabin, a steamboat shows the importance of the Missouri River. In the background, a train speeds across a track in front of a mountain range. Above the scene is a banner with Nebraska's state motto.

INDUSTRY

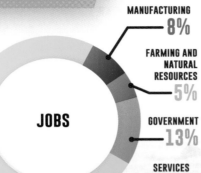

JOBS

MANUFACTURING
8%

FARMING AND
NATURAL
RESOURCES
5%

GOVERNMENT
13%

SERVICES
74%

Main Exports

medicine

beef

corn

pork

machinery

Natural Resources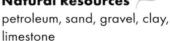
petroleum, sand, gravel, clay,
limestone

GOVERNMENT

Federal Government

3 | **2**
REPRESENTATIVES | SENATORS

NE

5
ELECTORAL
VOTES

USA

State Government

70 | **49**
REPRESENTATIVES | SENATORS

STATE SYMBOLS

STATE BIRD
WESTERN MEADOWLARK

STATE ANIMAL
WHITE-TAILED DEER

STATE FLOWER
GIANT GOLDENROD

STATE TREE
EASTERN COTTONWOOD

29

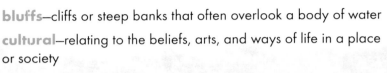

bluffs—cliffs or steep banks that often overlook a body of water

cultural—relating to the beliefs, arts, and ways of life in a place or society

Great Plains—a region of flat or gently rolling land in the central United States

heritage—the traditions, achievements, and beliefs that are part of the history of a group of people

immigrants—people who move to a new country

insurance—a business in which people pay money for protection against injuries or damages

Louisiana Purchase—a deal made between France and the United States; it gave the United States 828,000 square miles (2,144,510 square kilometers) of land west of the Mississippi River.

manufacturing—a field of work in which people use machines to make products

Midwest—a region of 12 states in the north-central United States

natural resources—materials in the earth that are taken out and used to make products or fuel

Oregon Trail—a route from Missouri to Oregon followed by westward settlers during the mid-1800s

powwow—a Native American gathering that usually includes dancing

prairie—a large, open area of grassland

reservations—areas of land that are controlled by Native American tribes

service jobs—jobs that perform tasks for people or businesses

settlers—people who move to live in a new, undeveloped region

traditional—related to customs, ideas, or beliefs handed down from one generation to the next

AT THE LIBRARY

Bodden, Valerie. *Sioux*. Mankato, Minn.: Creative Education, 2018.

Weber, Margaret. *Nebraska Cornhuskers*. New York, N.Y.: AV2 by Weigel, 2019.

Zeiger, Jennifer. *Nebraska*. New York, N.Y.: Children's Press, 2019.

ON THE WEB

FACTSURFER

Factsurfer.com gives you a safe, fun way to find more information.

1. Go to www.factsurfer.com.

2. Enter "Nebraska" into the search box and click 🔍.

3. Select your book cover to see a list of related content.

INDEX

The images in this book are reproduced through the courtesy of: Martin Hobelman, front cover, pp. 2–3; JIANG HONGYAN, p. 3 (corn); Stephanie Woolsey, pp. 4–5; Jim West/ Alamy, p. 5 (Ashfall Fossil Beds State Historical Park); Zack Frank, p. 5 (Chimney Rock); Michael Snell/ Alamy, p. 5 (Fort Kearny); Eric James/ Alamy, p. 5 (Henry Doorly Zoo and Aquarium); North Wind Picture Archives/ Alamy, p. 8; Krasnova Ekaterina, p. 9; Russ Bishop/ Alamy, p. 10 (Chimney Rock); Minerva Studio, p. 11; John McLaird, p. 11 (inset); Eric Isselee, p. 12 (timber rattlesnake); Holly S Cannon, p. 12 (coyote); Rick & Nora Bowers/ Alamy, p. 12 (Ord's kangaroo rat); Bruce MacQueen, p. 12 (wild turkey); moosehenderson, p. 12 (mountain lion); Sean Lema, p. 13 (black-tailed prairie dog); Paul Brady Photography, p. 14; NASA Image Collection/ Alamy, p. 15 (background); Wikipedia, p. 15 (Clayton Anderson); Danita Delimont, p. 16 (capitol building); Ryan McGinnis/ Alamy, p. 16 (rail yard); Jenn1030, p. 17 (Sunken Garden); Dani O'Brien, p. 18; Mark W Lucey, p. 19 (background); psgxxx, p. 19 (locking pliers); lovelyday12, p. 19 (Arbor Day); Helen Sessions / Alamy Stock Photo, p. 19 (Kool-Aid); mikeledray, p. 19 (frozen TV dinner); Brent Hofacker, pp. 20, 21 (runza, popcorn ball); Tendo, p. 21 (kernels); Cal Sport Media/ Alamy, pp. 22 (Omaha Storm Chasers), 23 (Cornhuskers); Anton N Bosschaert, p. 22 (rodeo); GILBERT MURRAY / Stockimo/ Alamy, p. 23 (Joslyn Art Museum); Mtsaride, p. 23 (football); shannonpatrick17/ Flickr, p. 24 (Czech Days); ZUMA Press, Inc./ Alamy, p. 24 (Winnebago Homecoming Powwow and Celebration); David7, pp. 26–27, 28–29, 30–31, 32; Bob Pool, p. 27 (1936); Mark W Lucey, p. 27 (2019); Millenius, p. 28 (flag); Magnetograph, p. 29 (western meadowlark); Jim Cumming, p. 29 (white-tailed deer); Przemyslaw Muszynski, p. 29 (giant goldenrod); K_E photography, p. 29 (eastern cottonwood); Tsekhmister, p. 31 (pig).